Y0-BOA-939

DAIRY COWS ON THE FARM

Cliff Moon

Illustrated by Anna Jupp

A DOWN ON THE FARM BOOK

THE BOOKWRIGHT PRESS
NEW YORK · 1983

Other books in this series

SHEEP ON THE FARM
POULTRY ON THE FARM
PIGS ON THE FARM

Published in the United States in 1983 by
The Bookwright Press, 387 Park Avenue South, New York NY 10016
First published in 1983 by
Wayland Publishers Ltd., England.
© Copyright 1983 Wayland Publishers Ltd

ISBN: 0-531-04695-8
Library of Congress Catalog Card Number: 83-71629
Printed in Italy by
G. Canale & C.S.p.A., Turin

Contents

Look at the picture.

This family is having breakfast.

They are putting milk on their cereal.

Milk comes from cows, and

this book is about cows.

5

Here are four kinds of cows.
Holstein and *Ayrshire* cows give a lot of milk.
Guernsey and *Jersey* cows
don't give so much milk, but
their milk is very creamy.

Guernsey

Ayrshire

Holstein

Jersey

7

It is summer, and the cows
can eat grass out in the fields.
In winter when the grass stops growing
the cows will eat hay.
Hay is dried grass.
What do you think the farmer is doing?
(Answer on page 32)

9

This cow has just had a baby calf.
The calf is drinking milk
from the cow's *udder*.
Now that the cow is making milk
for her calf, the farmer can begin
to collect her milk for us to drink.

These calves are a few days old.
They have to learn to eat on their own,
so the farmer mixes milk and other food
in buckets for them.

These cows have all had calves.
Their calves are eating the food
the farmer mixed for them.
So the cows are making milk but
they have no calves to feed.
Now the farmer can milk them.

Here are some cows being milked.

The machine sucks milk from the cows' udders.

Cows like being milked.

Can you think why?

(Answer on page 32)

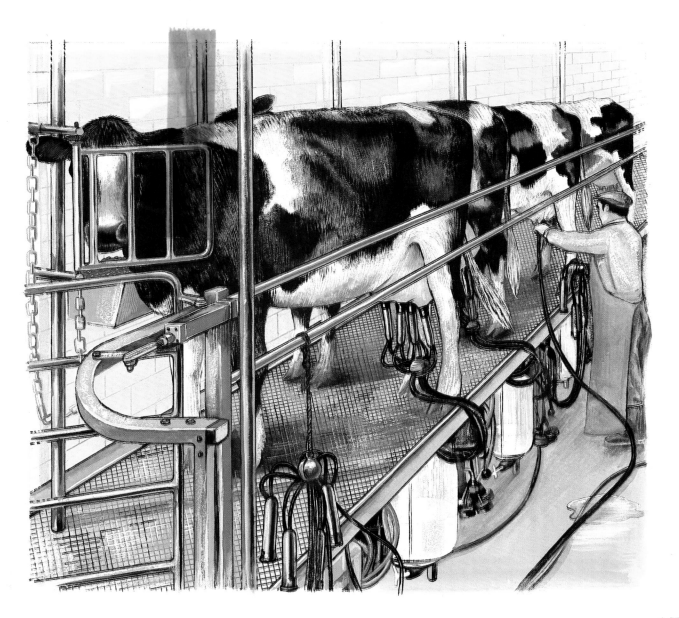

The machine has finished milking a cow.
The farmer is looking at
how much milk there is.
Every day he writes down
how much milk each cow gives.

pump

pipe

tank

measuring jar

19

A tank truck comes to the farm
to collect all the milk.
The milk goes along the pipe
into the tank.
The tank is cold, like a refrigerator.
Can you think why?
(Answer on page 32)

Now the tank truck is at the dairy.
The woman has taken some milk
from the tank, and she is making sure
that it is clean.
Next the milk will be made hot and
then cold again to kill all the germs.

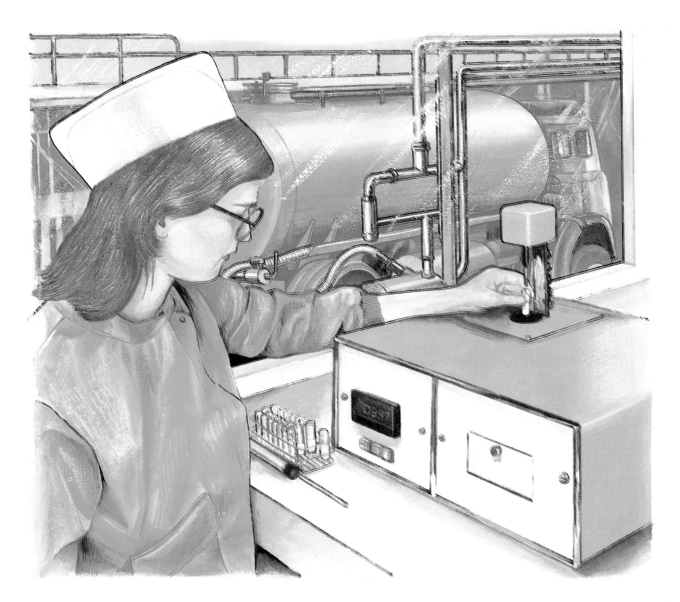

The milk is ready to drink, and
the machine is filling the bottles.
Every bottle has been washed
with hot and cold water.
How many bottles do you think
the machine can fill in one minute?
(Answer on page 32)

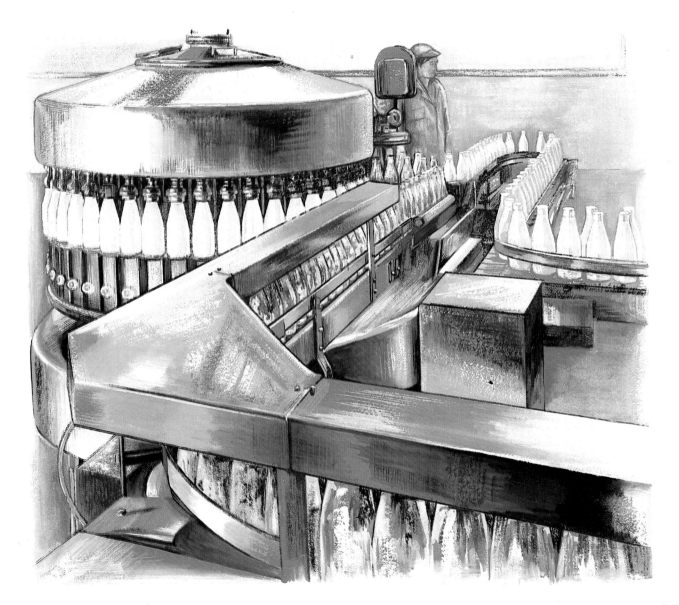

These calves are drinking milk,
like the calves on page 13.
But there is no cream in the milk.
The cream has been *skimmed* off the milk,
so this milk is called *skim milk*.

Butter and cheese are made from milk.
If you shake cream for a long time
it will turn into butter.
This machine has made cheese from milk.
How many different kinds of cheese
do you know?
They are all made from milk.

Here are the calves you saw on page 13.
Now they are growing up.
At first they stayed in a shed
near the farm.
Then they went out into the fields
to eat grass.
Soon they will be old enough
to have calves of their own.

31

Answers to questions

Page 8

The farmer is collecting hay.

He will keep it for the cows to eat in winter.

Page 16

Cows like being milked because their udders become full and uncomfortable.

Also they get special food at milking time.

Page 20

The tank is cold to keep the milk cool and fresh.

Page 24

The machine can fill and cap 600 milk bottles in one minute.

Index

AUG

NERL

f.
moon, Cliff
Dairy Cows on the
farm

OCT 27 2001